The Goodness of God

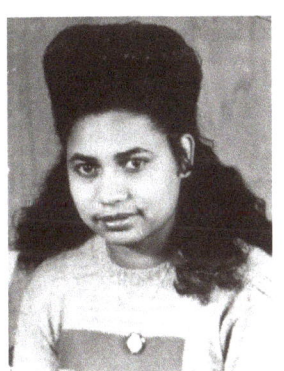

Bernette Majette Windom

World rights reserved. This book or any portion thereof may not be copied or reproduced in any form or manner whatever, except as provided by law, without the written permission of the publisher, except by a reviewer who may quote brief passages in a review.

The author assumes full responsibility for the accuracy of all facts and quotations as cited in this book. The opinions expressed in this book are the author's personal views and interpretations, and do not necessarily reflect those of the publisher.

This book is provided with the understanding that the publisher is not engaged in giving spiritual, legal, medical, or other professional advice. If authoritative advice is needed, the reader should seek the counsel of a competent professional.

Copyright © 2023 Bernette Majette Windom
Copyright © 2023 ASPECT Books
ISBN-13: 978-1-4796-1437-0 (Paperback)
Library of Congress Control Number: 2022902223

All scripture quotations, unless otherwise indicated, are taken from the King James Version (KJV) Public Domain.

Scripture quotations marked NJKV are taken from the New King James Version®. Copyright © 1982 by Thomas Nelson. Used by permission. All rights reserved.

Published by

Table of Contents

INTRODUCTION: Why This Book Was Written 5

STAGE 1: From Birth to Teenager. 7
STAGE 2: From Teenager to Young Adult 16
STAGE 3: From Young Adult to Middle Age. 25
STAGE 4: From Middle Age to Older Adult .31
STAGE 5: From Older Adult Forward 40

THE CONCLUSION 55

INTRODUCTION

Why This Book Was Written

First of all, I have been informed through different sources that our personal testimony, what God has done for us, is the greatest witnessing tool that we can use to reach people for God. This is why I am sharing with you how God has led, guided, and directed me through life with prayer, meditation, and reading the Bible, and focusing upon Him continuously. What He has done for me, He will do for you. God is no respecter of persons; He loves us all the same, and His desire is to save the whole world.

> I want to share a part in reaching the world for Christ. "Go ye therefore, and teach all nations, baptizing them in the name of the Father, and of the Son, and of the Holy Ghost: Teaching them to observe all things whatsoever I have commanded you: and, lo, I am with you always, even unto the end of the world. Amen. (Matt. 28:19–20)

I have a true passion for souls for Christ. If it were possible for me to get up on a house rooftop and shout out to the whole Christian world: "Satan has you deceived. You are going down the wrong path," I would do just that. Because I can't do that, I have decided to take a different route.

Satan knows that he has us if he can keep us deceived in honoring and worshipping God on the wrong day instead of the true Sabbath day. Just that alone can keep us out of the kingdom of God. The Bible tells us: "For whosoever shall keep the whole law, and yet offend in one point, he is guilty of all" (James 2:10). "But in vain they do worship me, teaching for doctrines the commandments of men" (Matt. 15:9).

Through much contemplation, I have decided, with the direction and help of God, to share my autobiography with the world. If I can reach just one soul for Christ, it will not have been in vain.

I would like to leave to my family and to the world a legacy that indicates what I believe, and in spite of all that I have gone through, who has been there for me in the time of need, and whenever I was going through the valley, and when all else failed, and who will also be there for you when you are going through your valley.

Finally, and for our own benefit, researchers at the universities of Wisconsin and Texas have proven that the act of telling our own history can lower our blood pressure, increase our self-esteem, and improve our immune system. According to Doug Batchelor, "God's message is our mission."

Please enjoy the reading of this book, and share it with a friend.

Author, Bernette Windom

STAGE 1

From Birth to Teenager

I am not a celebrity, a famous star, or a Hollywood icon. Instead, I am a conservative, modest person with the love of God in my heart.

I am taking you down a different path. Fasten your seatbelt, and hold on tightly. This path is rough and rugged.

My name is Bernette Majette Windom. I was born in Murfreesboro, North Carolina, on August 8, 1927. My parents were John Will Majette and Garrie Perry Majette. Both parents were descendants of mixed races; Black, White, Indian, and Irish ancestral lineage.

I am the fourth child of six siblings, the quiet, shy, and bashful one. I was a God-fearing child. I would check through the Bible when I could not read it and look at the pictures of God and His interaction with children and adults.

I have always wanted to have a part in God's eternal kingdom. I am sure that being raised in a home under the leadership and guidance of parents who were strict in their religious beliefs contributed a lot to this.

I remember my parents reading Bible stories to me, and I would phantom in my mind how I wanted to please God and be what He wanted me to be. I have often thought what a wonderful world this would be if we could maintain that childlike innocence, and come humbly before God with childlike faith, and trust Him totally and completely throughout our adult years.

When I was around three or four years old, I often heard older adults, my aunties, talking about their soul salvation and having to give an account for their sins. I distinctly heard them say, "We have to give an account for every strand of hair." As a child, I took that statement very seriously; I took it literally. I had a special place preserved underneath the house where I would place the hair combed from my head so I would know where to find it when the time came to give an account for it. That is how much I knew that I wanted to be saved eternally with God, even as a youngster. Can you imagine that?

Before I proceed further, perhaps I should give you a little background check on my parents. I have already given you their nationality roots.

My father and mother were both born and grew up in the town of Franklin, Virginia. Their parents were middle-class poor, not the poorest of poor or welfare poor, but poor enough. At the young age of ten years of age, my father moved to Murfreesboro, North Carolina, with the consent of his mother, to live with an uncle who didn't have any children. He requested that my father come to live with him to help him with his farming business. Uncle George had very little education. His reading and math was poor. He was getting ripped off in many ways; for example, when he took his cotton to the cotton gin to be weighed, he was told the cotton weighed whatever. Most of the time, it was everything but the number of pounds stated.

However, after my father went to live with Uncle George, everything took on a different outlook. My father was a great asset to his uncle. He helped him with his figuring and math, and when he took his cotton to the factory to be weighed, my father was there to verify the true amount the scales weighed in.

My father continued his education. After finishing elementary school, he continued and finished high school. Back in my father's day, a high school education was almost equivalent to a junior college education in this time span in which we're living.

After finishing high school, my father was drafted into the US Army during World War I at the age of eighteen. My father accomplished as much as the army allowed him at that time. He always talked about having worked in the mess hall as a cook. He was an excellent cook. He taught his daughters how to cook at an early age.

My dad said, "I didn't fight in the army because I carried my rifle in the opposite hand, contrary to the army's requirement."

My father was discharged from the First World War when he was in his twenties. He brought home with him the rules, regulations, and work schedule he had been taught in the army. He was a perfectionist. Everything had to be done just right, perfect, and exactly on his time schedule; otherwise, Mom was in trouble big time.

My father made the mistake of taking my mother captive at an early age, around fifteen years of age, due to the fact that her older sister, the love of his life, whom he had dated previously before entering the army, met and decided to marry another young man while my dad was still in the army.

When my dad got out of the army, he went to my mother's father, Grandpa Perry, and asked if he could marry my mother. Apparently, he felt he just had to have a Perry girl. However, young women did marry at an early age back in those days. Actually, this made my mom a victim of circumstances and possibly, at times, reaped the bitterness of not being the person of first choice.

Farm House I was born and raised in.

My father took my mother to this huge farm in North Carolina that he inherited from his uncle George. There the six of us were born. Unfortunately, it turned into somewhat of a dysfunctional family. After my mother's last child was born at the age of twenty, she had to have a total abdominal hysterectomy. The doctor didn't want her to bear or have any more children. My mother also suffered from postpartum syndrome. Instead of getting better, it escalated as time passed on. From this time forward, my mother was in a mental state of depression, and she was in and out of the hospital at intervals. We were basically raised by my father due to my mom's illness.

My mother's grandfather was a white man, and her grandmother was an Indian. My mother was a very quiet person. After doing some research and background checking, it was discovered that the Indian tribe that she was a descendant of was also a very quiet and reserved people.

My dad was just the opposite of my mother. He was a very talkative and outgoing person. He enjoyed associating and communing with older people. Although my mother was not talkative, she had a God-given gift of playing the piano. She could really make a piano talk, and she really loved doing that. At different times, she played for the Baptist Church's choir, which we grew up attending.

My father was a singer. He had a beautiful bass voice. He sang in the church's choir, and quite often, he sang solos for special music during the eleven o'clock service. He also taught the adult Sunday School class for many years, and he was also the church clerk for many years. He was very active in his church until his health declined. Both parents passed away in 1975. My mother died in May of 1975 at the age of sixty-seven. My father died in July of 1975 at the age of eighty-two. I am looking forward to being reunited with my parents in heaven.

Getting back to my early years, I learned at the age of four that the reason for rising early in the morning before the sun rose was to go to the cucumber field in my bare feet to pick the cucumbers while the vines were still wet with the morning dew. It was all about preserving the cucumbers.

However, as a kid, I determined in my mind when I grew up, I would never accept a job that required me to work early in the morning before the sun comes up. Guess what? For most of my working years, I worked either an afternoon or midnight shift, except for periods of orientation when I was required to work the day shift. What horrible stigma early rising put in my mind? The idea of getting up early in the morning to go to the job seemed to have caused frustrations. I felt as though I was being punished instead of looking forward with great anticipation of getting to the job. I also sensed a feeling of boredom and depression.

Nonetheless, the early rising, the chores, and all of the work experience contributed to my gaining the knowledge of responsibility at an early age. That is the good news, indeed.

As a youngster living at home with my parents, I knew nothing about having to provide for myself. I didn't have anything to be concerned about because my parents took care of all my needs; however, I did have different chores to do in order to keep up and maintain the household and take care of the animals.

The special chore assigned to me by my father was to take care of the chickens that were raised to produce eggs for the market. I had to grind the corn, feed the chickens, and water them. I also had to go to the forest and collect the needles from the pine trees to place in the hens' nests to protect the eggs from cracking or breaking when the hens laid them. Every evening at dusk, I had to collect the eggs before the chickens went in to sleep. I had to crate up all of the eggs in a huge wooden box and have them ready for sale at the end of each week.

I enjoyed all of the work. I enjoyed being around the chickens, watching them eat and be happy. It all gave me a sense of self-worth and self-esteem to be able to accomplish that specific chore for my dad. It truly was a rewarding experience. Those were the good days.

At age six, I was so excited about coming of age to attend school. I looked forward to being around other kids that were my age. However, as a black child growing up in the South, first of all, my siblings and I had to walk approximately five miles on a dirt road and partly-wooded area to a country school.

> *I enjoyed all of the work. I enjoyed being around the chickens, watching them eat and be happy. It all gave me a sense of self-worth and self-esteem.*

Our white peers rode a school bus. On our way to school with other kids who lived in our country area, the white kids in their bus passed us, ran us off the road, dusted us, and peered their head out the window and called us, you know what? Yes, "little black niggers." Eventually, the county provided a school bus for black children who lived in my area to be taken into the town of Murfreesboro to school.

Fortunately, my oldest brother was able to get the job of driving the bus.

Not only were we harassed by children of our opposite race, but we were also looked upon by our neighbors as being inferior to them. My father owned his farm, and we had the same things they had. In fact, my father's farm was much larger than either of theirs. Our surrounding neighbors were three white farmers who were brothers. Charlie, Tom, and George Benson. My father would always refer to them as Mr. Charlie, Mr. Tom, and Mr. George, and he taught us to do the same. They never once called my father Mr. John, nor did any of their children. Their children always called my father John as though he was another child. This puzzled me until I was old enough to understand what the deal was. Then it became humiliating.

In spite of all the humiliations and segregation, my kindergarten and elementary schooling was very enjoyable. I had a very devoted, kind, and loving teacher, Mrs. Purdy. She spent a lot of time with me inside the classroom as well as in her home. She asked my father if I could come and spend time with her. I spent weeks with her at intervals. She probably would have adopted me if my father would have consented. She was like a mother to me. She had recently married at that time, but she didn't have any children. I will always remember her. She was a gem, very special.

The first thing that excited me about elementary school was I liked spelling. I could spell any word without problems. When I graduated from the seventh grade to enter high school, I was honored as salutatorian of my class.

The second thing that excited me when I was in the seventh grade, the principal of the school sponsored a trip for my class to visit the US Capitol in Washington, D.C.

We got to explore the entire Capitol building from the first floor to the top of the building. I can't remember how many stories high it was, but it was so high that when we looked down to the ground, the moving cars looked like little tiny play cars that boys get at Christmas time.

We also got to visit the room where the US money is printed and watched the machines as they printed out new paper money.

We visited the entire area where the president lived at that time, however, just from the outside of the building.

It was an exciting, memorable experience.

The negative things that seemed to penetrate my life as I grew into my adolescent and teen years were being fearful, shy, and bashful. I was fearful of what would happen to my mother because her health had started declining. I was very concerned about her. I wanted her to be able to stay at home with us children. I didn't know exactly how to pray, but I prayed honestly in the way that I knew to pray at that time. "Dear God, please save my mother, please heal her, and please protect her. But if it's in her best interest not to live at home, Dear God, let Your will be done."

Unfortunately, another tragic situation transpired in my life when I was eight years old. Our attention is focused on my younger brother. nine years of age, whose name was Clarence Socrates. We called him Sock. He was a very adorable child. He was talkative, and he had a great sense of humor. He was constantly saying something to make you laugh. He was very funny. Sock was also explorative. He liked to check out the things around him and find out how they operated and what they were made of.

Sock and our siblings had permission from Dad to explore the entire farm. But we did not have permission to go beyond the borders of the farm. On the east side of the farm was a creek. On the opposite side of the creek was another farm. The owner of that farm decided to cut timber. You could hear him from a long distance cutting the trees, and finally, the tree would fall, and the machine would stop for a few minutes.

Sock was curious and anxious to find out how that giant machine operated. He had to find a way to get to the machine so he could see for himself exactly how it worked. Finally, one day he came up with an idea.

The family had lunch every day at noon. After lunch, our dad would take an hour for nap time, and Mother would take this time to help my older sister with her sewing. Sock decided this would be the perfect time to take off and explore the giant timber machine. Without getting permission from our parents, he talked my younger two sisters and me into going with him on this adventurous trip; however, we had to cross a creek to get to the machine. Sock thought the water was shallow enough to walk or wade across to the opposite side. He decided to go across first, and we were to follow after he had crossed over.

Sock got about midway of the creek, and suddenly, his head went under the water. I shouted, "Sock, Sock, what is wrong?? Sock, can you hear me?" He did not answer. Again, his head went under the water and came up. The third time his head went under the water, he never came up again.

Yes, my precious, special little brother drowned at nine years of age, and I was eight years old.

It took a long time to ward off that devastating tragedy. I found out the hard way as a child that children are not to go anyplace without the permission of parents.

I was overwhelmed; my life was shattered. It was difficult to find closure and get on with my life. I felt guilty. I felt that I contributed to my brother's death by not consulting our parents about the situation and what we wanted to do. I could not let go until I had grown older, gotten married, and given birth to my five children. I was so busy trying to raise and take care of them that is when I stopped worrying about my brother's death. Thank God, something finally brought closure.

In spite of all that I went through as a youngster, being discriminated against because of the color of my skin, my mother's health problems, and the death of my brother, I recognized I still had to keep moving forward, attending school. It was difficult because I didn't get the love and support I needed from my mother. I felt that something was missing or lacking. I felt cheated out of something because my mother was not there with me. I could not perceive a future filled with hope. Anxiety and fear had its grip on me, preventing me from being self-confident and having definite plans and objectives for my life.

Assuredly, I always liked school and enjoyed it very much. I never missed or skipped a day except for one time when I was in high school. I skipped school so I could ride the bike that my three sisters and I had to share. I wanted a little more bike time. I loved riding my bike even into my senior years.

STAGE 2

From Teenager to Young Adult

After finishing high school, I wanted to join the US Army (Second World War). I wanted to travel and also acquire an education so my father wouldn't have to bear the expenses. My oldest brother and sister were in college at that time. However, for whatever reason, my father talked me out of the military involvement.

I had a high school classmate who joined the army even though the war had ceased. At that time, in 1945, they were still recruiting volunteers. This young lady was trained and became a registered nurse. She never had to participate in the war's fighting. What a blessing.

Before moving forward regarding school, let me go back a bit to my home training. As a young teenager, my father kept my sisters and brothers and me involved in the church from a very early age to the late teen years. We had to attend church every Sunday whether we wanted to or not. If I played sick for not attending church, as far as my dad was concerned, I was too sick to even go out of the house all day. Church attendance entailed Sunday School study, the eleven) o'clock church service, a break for lunch, and then the young people's afternoon meeting. Lastly, a special singing program or professional concert was held at night.

Regarding lunch, most of the time, my dad would take us to one of his friends' home for lunch. I didn't like that. I'm shy and bashful, and I preferred going home for lunch. This all-day routine was for each and every Sunday. Guess what? I thought to myself, *If I ever get grown and leave this house, I will never go to church again*.

In our early teen years, my siblings and I had to do farm work as well as house chores. Back in that day, we had to chop the weeds and grass from all the planted crops with a hand-held hoe. My father planted a garden each year and raised all of the food that we ate, including the animal products. However, most of the animals he raised were for sale. He didn't believe in feeding us too much meat. He would tell us in plain and simple words. "Meat will make you dumb," I said, "I don't want to be dumb."

> *I thought to myself, If I ever get grown and leave this house, I will never go to church again.*

The two crops my father grew or raised for sale were cotton and peanuts. Can you believe it? I learned to pick cotton and stack peanuts at an early age. We had to shell all of the peanuts my father planted each year.

I also ate my share of peanuts. If I never eat anymore, I ate enough to last me a lifetime! My father also raised tobacco the last year of his farming. I learned how to prime tobacco from the field and loop it on sticks to be placed in a special barn to be cured at night.

My dad apparently had reached the boiling point. He couldn't go any further. He had to tend this huge farm with two mules and plows, and one of the mules was stubborn, from what I could see. My dad had to whip him

to get him going. By the time we all became older teens, my father decided to sell his farm. Guess what? The very year after selling the farm, a tractor was advertised for sale. If the tractor had been advertised a bit earlier, perhaps my dad could have held on a little longer.

My farm life was enjoyable; it was a healthy lifestyle. I learned how to work and how to be responsible. It was indeed an inspiring experience.

Coming back into the house from the farm, as early teenagers, my sisters and I could perform every household chore that any adult woman did: wash clothes, clean the entire house, cook meals, iron clothes. I had to wash and iron my dad's white shirts that he wore to church on Sunday without a spot or wrinkle. We had to pick, wash, and store fruits and vegetables in freezer jars for winter. We also stored potatoes in an outside pit to preserve for winter use.

Before selling the farm, my dad had decided to build us a new house. He consulted with some of the businessmen of the town, and they talked him out of the idea, giving him different excuses for not building, including an economic collapse. We were disappointed.

Also, prior to selling the farm, my father had timber cut from the forest and had houses built in the town of Murfreesboro and Ahoskie to rent. So, he decided to renovate one of the houses in our town of Murfreesboro for us to move into.

Now we were closer to our neighbors, our classmates, and our peers. I was in my later teens, and my father had become more restrictive regarding our association with others. Dating young men was totally out of the question for all of us.

Attending school and attending church was our routine. My dad involved my oldest sister and brother in his adult church choir. My sister had a high soprano voice, and my brother had a good baritone voice. My dad wanted me to play the piano because I had hands and long fingers like my mother's. He thought that my hands were designed to play the piano. He had me sitting at the piano going over the keyboard at three years of age. I didn't want to play the piano. Can you imagine—I wanted to sing, yes, sing. My dad didn't spend time with me singing; however, I did sing in the youth choir for a short time, after which I organized a singing group with my younger two sisters and me.

We did quite a bit of singing in our church, but we never sang in school. We sang during intermission for the offering at different programs and concerts. At one specific time, a family-organized men's quartet, four brothers, presented a program at our church, and we sang during the intermission for the offering. They were so excited about our singing and liked it so well that they wanted us to come and sing with them on their radio program. Back in that day, we didn't have the TV and different programs being televised. We felt it was truly a blessing to be able to sing over the radio. Guess what? When we shared the information with my dad, he said, "No way."

I thought this would be an opportunity to help improve our singing. On the contrary, my dad probably thought it would lead to our detriment and involvement in the things of the world. I loved singing, and it broke my heart when Dad said no. I was so disappointed, I gave up singing at that time and started focusing on furthering my education in college.

My dad always had such strict guidelines and rules for our life, my sisters and me, but he and his friends appeared to be having a ball, a good time doing whatever they wanted to do. That puzzled me. I was watching these adults and thinking my dad should be setting an example for us and restrict himself as well.

My dad smoked cigarettes; unfortunately, he took on the habit while in the army. He did not drink alcohol, but he had a close friend who drank alcohol. The pastor of our church also smoked cigarettes.

I began to wonder if I was in the right church. I started praying earnestly about the situation, asking God to reveal to me the church organization that lived according to the Bible and what they preached.

When I began college, I was motivated to attend Bennett College in Greensboro, North Carolina. This was an all-women's Methodist college, within walking distance across from A&T College, which was co-ed, where my brother and sister were attending. Being bashful, shy, and quiet, I did not want to attend college with the boys. Apparently, God was leading and directing me to Bennett College.

Let me back up a bit regarding college. There was a beautiful college in my hometown of Murfreesboro, not far from our house. Guess what? Yes, you know, we could not attend this college because of the color of our skin. This was Chowan College. If we could have attended this college, we could have stayed at home and received our education instead of going away to a boarding college. It would have been much easier on my father financially. Having three children in college at the same time was a heavy load for him.

Getting back to Bennett College, it consisted mostly of white women at this particular time. Being a church college is probably the only reason blacks could attend. The schools in the South had not yet been integrated. Within the entire population of Bennett College, I encountered only one young Black woman. Her name was Glennie Rucker. Guess what? She was a member of the Seventh-day Adventist Church. She told me about this church and that they believed in going strictly by the Bible and living their life accordingly. She also told me about Ellen G. White, who was a prophetess.

I was so excited about all of the information she shared with me. I was overwhelmed. To top it off, she said, "Next semester, I'm going to Oakwood College." This is a Seventh-day Adventist College in Huntsville, Alabama. I thought about it and decided I wanted to go to this college and learn more about the Bible and this particular church organization. I said, "I'm going to ask my dad if I can go, and he would probably say no," He said yes, so then I could go to Oakwood College.

On the train to Oakwood College in 1947, I met Elder Charles D. Brooks. He was seventeen years of age at that time. I never would have imagined he would become a world-famous evangelistic minister for God. However, God can perform outstanding and marvelous works through an open and willing heart.

When I arrived on those grounds at Oakwood College, I could sense the sacredness of the atmosphere and the grounds. I felt like I was walking on holy ground. I visited the college twice in my adult years. Each time I was there, I felt the same sacredness of those grounds. I concluded it is definitely a God-chosen school.

During my time at Oakwood, I was able to get into an in-depth study of the Bible. Elder H.M.S. Richards was my Bible instructor. After learning more about the Bible and God's will for my life, I decided to get re-baptized into the Seventh-day Adventist Church at eighteen years of age.

I enjoyed my studies, and I liked the way the entire facility operated and the activities planned for the students on Saturday nights after the Sabbath. No dancing with the young men, instead they allowed marches performed in a single line with one person, not a couple, and the music was modest.

Behold, I was introduced to vegetarian food, and I actually enjoyed it. Having been raised on a farm, my dad did not feed us a lot of flesh food. We ate a lot of vegetables. He would always tell us, "Meat will make you dumb." I was able to adjust to the diet fairly well.

Most of all, I enjoyed the Sabbath service and youth choir. They did a fantastic job. I looked forward to hearing them each Sabbath.

I felt that I was out in the world all alone until I came to the Lord at Oakwood. I was so concerned for my mother's health that I could not properly focus and concentrate on what I was obligated to do.

Another thing that concerned me at that time was the fact that I didn't have the proper clothing needed for attending boarding school. My father was determined to educate us, but he didn't think we needed any clothes or anything else we wanted or needed; that it would put a damper on our wanting to get an education so we could properly take care of ourself.

There was no such thing as a government grant or loan for college in those days. If we could have gone to Chowan College, it would have been much simpler and much cheaper for my father to educate us.

Being black in this world has not been easy, especially being raised in the South, experiencing first-hand prejudice. I believe this is the reason we are not bonded as a race because so much hatred, bitterness, injustice,

> *I felt that I was out in the world all alone until I came to the Lord at Oakwood.*

and prejudice has been directed toward us as a race until we don't like ourselves, and in some cases, we don't like each other as a whole. I believe the system was designed to destroy us mentally, physically, emotionally, and socially, as well as financially.

For the most part, or may I say as a whole, the black race has been a survivor, strong and determined to be an overcomer. Our black men and women have moved forward in spite of the stigma attached to them. They have done exceedingly well, however, not given the credit in many cases.

But what about the weaker ones? Those who were raised up in a home without strong back support from a strong and determined father and mother. Every human being is different. What affects one in a drastic way may not even affect another the same way.

Having been born and raised in a system and society that is designed and programmed against blacks has driven so many of our black men down the path of destruction. I believe that drugs were legally permitted into this country to target and destroy our young black men. Not knowing what was happening, they fell for the drugs like a ton of brick.

First of all, the drugs give them a quick fix. They use them to go on a high and forget their problems for a minute and probably feel better about themselves than ever before. They don't worry about what they don't have, and they want to keep it that way. The drugs lead them into a continuous usage—a habit.

They are in a stupor, unable to think for themselves, unable to make the right choices. The drugs destroy their mind, body, and soul. They become unable to do anything constructive for themselves. This is where the system designed them to be—sitting in a stupor, going no place, doing nothing but more drugs.

My heart goes out to our young black men. I wish I could tap them one by one, and wake them up, and let them know you have fallen for a trap. Wake up; don't be scooped in. Wake up and live, go back to school. Get your GED so you can prepare yourself for a skill, a trade, a profession, something that can provide you a legal, legitimate, adequate-paying job.

Get off the streets peddling drugs, or you will eventually end up dead or in jail. The system will consume you in one way or another. There is no such thing as quick money or money overnight. Nothing is free in this world, and everything that is illegal comes with a penalty. We are to obey the laws of the land as well as God's laws. The Bible tells us, "The wages of sins is death." I say to our young black men, do not let Satan deceive you into destroying your mind, body, and soul. Then he has you exactly where he likes you to be. You have lost out in this world, and you have lost out in eternal life. If we miss out on eternity, we will have missed everything.

God tells us, "But seek ye first the kingdom of God, and his righteousness; and all these things shall be added unto you" (Matt. 6:33). He will provide us with what we need if we will submit to Him in faith. He provides for the sparrows and the birds of the air; how much more will He provide for us humans, whom He created in His own image and likeness? God loves us so much, according to His Word. We will be studying and learning about God and His love for us throughout the ceaseless ages of eternity. Again, to our young black men, do not be deceived by Satan; God has something better in store for you.

The one thing that comes to my mind each year during Black History Month, is the fact of having been discriminated against regarding the pursuing of an education.

Sorry, I got swept away by prejudice and racial injustice. But now I'm back at Oakwood. I found out that the college sponsored an evangelistic program, soliciting volunteers during summer vacation to go to different areas of the country to sell religious magazines and books in order to earn a scholarship.

I thought if I could earn a scholarship to pay my tuition, then my dad could buy me some clothes. So, I decided to go with the evangelistic program. When the sponsors of the program began calling off the different states that we could go to New York, California, Ohio, Detroit, Mich. When I heard the word Detroit, I said, "That's it; that is where I want to go." I had been longing to visit Detroit, Michigan, ever since I was a youngster.

My dad had a cousin who lived in Detroit. My dad's sister, Auntie Arleean's husband unfortunately, got killed in the First World War. She then traveled quite often from Franklin, Virginia, to Detroit, Michigan, to visit this cousin. She also visited Canada. She would visit us kids afterward and tell us about Detroit and Canada. She made it so exciting that I said, "One day, I would like to go to Detroit and Canada." This was the key for me wanting to solicit the Detroit area.

I met a young lady while at Oakwood College. Mary Tillman, who was from Kansas City, Missouri. She also decided to partake in the evangelistic program. She and I left Oakwood College together and came to Detroit, Michigan, in the summer of 1948 to work on a scholarship.

The leaders of the program also provided housing for us in the homes of Christian people who were affiliated with City Temple SDA Church. We worked under the leadership of a young man from the Lake Region Conference. Yes, we worked. I met Catherine Neal at this time. She came from Andrews University to also work on a scholarship.

We went from door to door in different areas of Detroit. We canvassed on different streets. We even canvassed Hastings Street, which was considered one of the most dangerous areas of Detroit. We also went to the Ford Motor Company.

Guess what? I walked my feet to a size and a half larger shoe during that summer, but, sad to say, I did not earn a scholarship. So, what's next? I did not want to go back to boarding school without proper or sufficient clothing. At this particular time, I was living with the Thomas family. Brother Thomas was the head elder at the City Temple SDA Church. Sister Thomas indicated I would have to get permission from my father if I did not go back to Oakwood College in order to continue living with them. I talked to my father, and he consented for me to stay in Detroit.

I applied for a job at Grace Hospital on John R Street in Detroit, Michigan. I was hired and trained as a nurse's aide.

STAGE 3

From Young Adult to Middle Age

During this time, I met a very nice gentleman through some church friends. After working at Grace Hospital for about two years, we were married. This man had a sparkling personality and a great sense of humor. He was six feet tall and the most good-looking man I had ever seen. No kidding!

We started our family shortly, which consisted of five children, three sons and two daughters. My dad would always kid me about having a lot of children when I was older and married. It was interesting to note; he never kidded my sisters regarding this issue. He would compare me with the old lady who lived in a shoe, and she had so many children she didn't know what to do. I thought to myself, *poor lady*, I felt so sorry for her. At other times, my dad would come to me and ask the question, "Old lady, old lady, how much will you ask for your daughter?" He would answer the question. "Fifteen cents and a dollar and a quarter."

As a kid, I could not figure out why my father would kid me about having a lot of children, but after having five children, I thought Dad was right on target. I ended up with more children than any of my siblings, a houseful. Truly, I was the old lady who lived in the shoe; however, the shoe was my father- and mother-in-law's house.

My husband was an only child. He was very close to his mother. I could not get him to move out of their home until the fourth child was born. The babies forced him to move out. There was no more room in the shoe!

I enjoyed being a wife for my husband, and I enjoyed raising our five children. We had a lot of fun together. My husband most definitely loved his children dearly, and he had a deep, protective concern for their welfare. He spent a lot of time with them. He engaged his sons in the sports that he enjoyed. He was always willing to give counsel to the girls and the boys when necessary.

For our twenty-fifth wedding anniversary, my husband bought me my first automobile. So, we decided to do a little more exploring of Canada rather than just crossing the bridge from Detroit into Canada. My husband drove my new car, and we went quite a long distance into Canada, spending three days and nights there. We returned home by crossing over the Ambassador Bridge into the US and Detroit. I really enjoyed this trip; however, the problem that took its grip on me was I didn't speak the French language fluently. I remembered a little of my high school French at that time.

Getting back to my husband and our kids, he talked about something regarding the children the entire time we were in Canada. No matter where we were, he would discuss something about our children. I said, "Bill, I thought we left the children at home." His name was Willie, but I always called him Bill. It was our time to get a short break; instead, he took them with us. This is how much he loved our children. My husband was a loving, devoted husband, father, and grandfather. I worked all of the years of my marriage except for one short time that I decided to take one year off from work in order to spend more time with my children in their formative and sensitive years.

I had no problem working because I always wanted to have my own money and not have to give an account and keep a record of every penny that I spent and what I spent it for. OK? Often, I look back and wonder how did I work all those years, having five children and a working husband. It had to be God who brought me through. Amen?

> *My husband was a loving, devoted husband, father, and grandfather.*

I always had two babies in diapers at the same time. I would be up all night at intervals changing diapers and feeding bottles, then arise at 6:00 a.m., prepare breakfast for my husband, and pack his lunch so he could get to work. Later, I would go to work.

My second helper was my mother-in-law. Clara Windom was a gem. She was like a mother to me. After retiring from her job, she was basically my babysitter for all of my working years. She loved her grandchildren and would do any and everything to help provide for their needs. They spent more time at her home than they did at their home. When I had a few days off from work to spend with them, she would call to find out if they could come to be with her. She never appeared to get tired or bored by taking care of them. Actually, I think if it were possible for her to do so, she would have adopted them.

When my oldest son became a teenager and was going through that rebellious stage of his life, he decided to leave home and go to live with his grandparents. Apparently, he felt like they were his parents also. It broke my heart. Nonetheless, they were precious.

My father-in-law, J.C. Windom, was a tall six-footer, laid-back type of person, and very humorous. He was very good at helping his wife, Clara, with the care of the children and the training and disciplining as well. He always called me daughter.

My mother-in-law was always right by my side regardless of what transpired in my marriage. I have to be honest; at times, I had to get busy fighting off other women, not physically but mentally. I was determined, no, you can't have him. Thank God, before it was too late, things were resolved, confessions were made, forgiveness granted, and happy ever after.

This brings to remembrance a letter that my dad wrote to me after my marriage in 1952. Can you imagine a seven-page letter?? Titled quote, "Keep him courting you." He strongly recommended that women stop fooling themselves by going to trick doctors and magicians to keep their husbands at home. It takes the same thing to keep your husband that it took to get him. Keep yourself neat, trim, and presentable exactly as you did when you were expecting a proposal from him. The woman who takes her husband for granted will soon no longer have a husband.

Do not argue with your husband. A clever woman has many ways of attaining her ends, and arguing is surely not one of the ways.

Do not be quick to blame your husband even if it is his own fault. You are to be his helpmate, a pal, not a critic. When things go wrong, that is when he needs your sympathetic understanding and comfort. You never help a man by kicking him when he is down.

Don't ask your husband where he was or who he was with when he comes home late at night. If you wait, he will tell you. No man likes to face a cross-examination every time he comes home from a meeting with his friends. You may be as clever as a lawyer, but your husband is not the person on whom to practice.

Never accuse your husband of things that he is not guilty of. If you do, it won't be long before he will quit you from lying.

Don't be a grouch, don't be a crank, do not complain. Your husband has his own problems at his work. Each profession and each type of work has its own problems. He wants to forget them when he comes home. He expects you to meet him with a smile, cheerful words, and have something interesting to tell him. If you let him down or disappoint him, he will look elsewhere for understanding and sympathy. He will find it in some woman.

Have your husband's meals prepared on time. Don't keep him waiting for his dinner. Try to cook his food the way he likes it. Don't tell him he should be glad to get it any way he can.

If he should or happen to come home after mealtime, don't call him to his meal and then leave him. That reminds him of the way you feed the cats and dogs. Stay with him until he finishes his meal to see that he has plenty.

Always prepare something that he especially likes to eat, without him having to tell you. That will at least make him feel that you are interested in and concerned about him.

This particular section of my father's letter reminds me of an experience I had in preparing a meal for my husband. In our early marriage, approximately three times yearly, he would ask me to cook neck bones and pig's feet. I knew that swine's flesh was unclean meat. Actually, I didn't want to touch it, much less cook it. However, being his wife, I felt obligated to cook it for him. I would wash it thoroughly, season it well, and cook it until the meat was falling off the bone. I wanted to make sure it was cooked to the fullest. After eating, he would always say to me, "Bernette, those were some good neck bones and pig's feet."

During this time, I had been witnessing to him concerning the clean and the unclean meats. I told him exactly where to find the information in the Bible, so he could read it for himself in his leisure time. After reading it in the book of Leviticus, chapter eleven of the Bible, he came to me again with the neck bones and pig's feet to cook for him. I cooked it the exact same way. After eating it, he came to me and said, "Bernette, the neck bones and pig's feet made me sick." Guess what? My husband never asked me to cook him any more neck bones and pig's feet.

I thought to myself, *Wow, that was God's way of telling him it's time to let the unclean meat go because you have read it for yourself, and now you know it's unclean.* God doesn't hold us accountable for what we don't know, but He holds us accountable for what we do know. God is awesome. He has His way of reaching us in whatever situation we're facing or experiencing.

In the final stage of my dad's letter, he told me, "Do not allow people to bring you news about your husband. If they once find out that you are a garbage can, they will keep you filled up. Don't talk about your husband's shortcomings or problems to other people."

My father states, "I have tried to outline a few of the highlights on keeping your husband, and keeping him happy and interested in you." "Try them if you are interested in making your married life a permanent courtship. They will pay you dividends in happiness and contentment."

STAGE 4

From Middle Age to Older Adult

Getting back to my in-laws, as they began to grow older, their physical health started to gradually decline. My mother-in-law had to make a lot of visits to doctors. I am thankful that I was able to take her to her various doctor visits.

During this time, my father-in-law had a slight stroke, and he had to walk with a cane, but he could get around in his house.

At this point in my life, all of my children were teenagers, and I had become more involved in church activities. I sang in the adult choir, and I was a Sabbath School assistant superintendent, working under the supervision of Inez Shelton, the principal of Peterson Warren Academy at that time. I was also a deaconess. Most of all, I worked with Minnie White in giving Bible studies to individuals. My in-laws consented to take Bible studies. That was an exciting, delightful experience.

After they completed the studies, Pastor C.S. Lewis came and interviewed them to find out if they had any questions about what they had studied. Apparently, they were content with what they had learned. Pastor Lewis asked them if they were willing to get baptized. They both consented; however, their physical health prevented them from getting into the water. Pastor Lewis stated, "After agreeing to get baptized even though they could not physically get into the water, it was as if they did."

Shortly afterward, my mother-in-law's health started to worsen to the extent of having to have a home care nurse come in or go to a nursing home. Clara Windom did not want to go to a nursing home. So, I decided to take a nine-month leave of absence from my job in order to care for her and my father-in-law, J.C. Windom, in their home. I cleaned the house, washed their clothes, and prepared their food. I had to give Clara her baths from her bed. She was a large, tall woman. It was a struggle to get her out of bed after her baths, but with God's help, I did.

After the nine months, I had to return to my job. Clara had a home care nurse come in for about a month, and then her doctor hospitalized her. She was admitted to the hospital where I was working, and guess what? On the same floor where I worked, on the unit around the corner from my desk.

I could see her call light over her room door when it came on. If it were not answered right away, I would leave my desk and go to her room to take care of her needs.

I visited her during my break time and often while on duty. When Clara Windom passed away, I was there in her room along with her oldest grandson. When the last breath went out of her body, the biggest smile came over her face. I suddenly looked around to see if Frank saw that big beautiful smile, and when I looked back at her, she and the smile was gone. I had never experienced anything like that. However, that big smile motivated me into thinking my mother-in-law is at peace with God. Praise the Lord.

> *When the last breath went out of her body, the biggest smile came over her face.*

My mother-in-law's death had a terrible impact on my husband's life and health. He had a very close relationship with his mother. At one time, he stated, "I hope that I pass away before my mother. I don't think I can handle or survive her passing."

During the grieving process, he was trying to stand strong before his three teenage sons. Actually, he was holding his grieving inward instead of crying out loud. They put their arms around him and said, "Dad, it's alright, OK to cry; let it out." He did not, and, sad to say, he had an asthma attack.

I took him to different doctors trying to get help as the problem escalated. I made an appointment with a different doctor, who was a specialist in his particular problem.

I was about to walk out of the house to take him for his appointment. He was waiting in the living room while I ran into the bedroom to grab my purse. Suddenly, I heard him fall to the floor. Right away, I called 911. He was saying, "I'm not going to make it; I can't breathe." I said, "Yes, Bill, you are going to make it; when the emergency squad get here, they will have equipment to help you breathe."

They came right away, hooked him up, put him on the stretcher, and took him to the ambulance. Can you believe it? While they were moving him inward, he moved his hand as if he were saying goodbye to me. I followed the ambulance to the hospital. When I went into the emergency room, they gave me the sad news that my husband, Willie Windom, passed away on the way to the hospital, which was on September 19, 1984.

What a tragic experience! I did not realize his illness was that severe since he kept on working. He worked for Ford Motor Co. for thirty-eight years.

I was so frustrated over his death that I began trying to work things out on my own instead of turning the situation totally and completely over to God and praying and trusting Him to bring me through. Yes, I had a close relationship with God but, not nearly as close as I am today. Thank You, Lord, that You have promised in Your Word that "You will never leave us nor forsake us" (see Heb. 13:5).

I went for counseling, thinking that would bring me through. I even went back to work instead of taking the time allotted to me for this particular situation. I felt that I would be more comfortable around people rather than being at home alone. That did not work. I felt really bad after grieving and crying around my co-workers. I decided to take the time from work given to me.

My heavenly Father was trying to let me know that He was right by my side, and He would bring me through. I could sense His presence. However, I was still trying to work out the situation on my own.

After taking the allotted time off from work and then returning to work on the afternoon shift, I was feeling much better and relaxed. Can you imagine? One morning, I awakened to go to the bathroom, and everything in the living room—the whole room—glittered with extreme brightness. I had to check it out. Guess what? The front door to my house was standing wide open—not a small crack but opened as far back as it could go. Do you think I would go to sleep late at night and leave my front door open? No way! I felt that God was again trying to get my attention. Sometimes He has to break us in order to make us. God spoke to me later in clear words. "I'm right by your side. Wasn't I there to protect you when your door was standing open?"

I'm still trying to work things out instead of relying totally upon my God. I was listening to the news channel prior to Easter, and they were announcing that a tour to the Holy Land was scheduled to take place for Easter hosted by two ministers in Southfield, Michigan.

I began thinking if I could get over to the Holy Land and walk on the grounds where Jesus walked, everything would be resolved. Guess what? I was able to make the proper contacts and, with God's help, go on the three-week tour to the Holy Land in the spring of 1985. I was very excited and anxious to get there and see that part of the world.

All of the people on the tour were Christians from different denominations. The youngest person in the group was my roommate. She was a devoted Christian, well-versed in the Bible. We had a sixteen-hour flight

across the Atlantic Ocean from New York to Cairo, Egypt. We made one stop for refueling in Vienna, Austria. Then we spent five days in Egypt before going to Israel.

I visited the Egyptian Museum and the wooden factory where rugs are made by hand. I visited the papyrus factory, where different things are made from the papyrus plant. I also visited the Valley of the Kings, where the tombs of the pharaohs and queens of Egypt are located. I also experienced the excitement of climbing one of the tallest pyramids of Egypt on the Sahara Desert and the fun of riding a camel's back.

We left Egypt and went to Israel. I visited most of the places that the Bible speaks of concerning where Jesus lived, walked, and went. We stayed in a hotel on top of the Mount of Olives.

I rode down the sea of Galilee, crossed over to Capernaum and to the Mount of the Beatitudes. I went to Jerusalem and down the Via Dolorosa, the path that Jesus walked and carried His cross to be crucified. I visited the Garden of Gethsemane, the garden tomb where Jesus was buried. I also went to Bethlehem to the site where Jesus was born. A church is built over the site now, called the Church of the Nativity. I also went to Nazareth, where Jesus lived with His parents until He began his ministry. I also visited the city of Jericho, which is the oldest city in the world. Lastly, I drank water from the original Jacob's Well.

We left Israel and went to Jordan, the land of ancient treasures and modern pleasures. We spent five days there. We visited the City of Amman, and I rode horseback from Amman to the ancient city of Petra.

I spent twenty-two exciting days walking in the footsteps of Jesus and other places abroad. This gave me a sense of renewed hope, a spiritual renewal and revitalization, and, most of all, a new meaning of the Holy Bible and its teachings. However, the highlight of my tour was getting rebaptized in the Jordan River, where Jesus was baptized by John the Baptist. I can honestly say it all was a wonderful and rewarding experience.

When I returned home, I started grieving again. God spoke to me. He said, "Your husband has been deceased more than a year; it's time for you to come out of the grieving process. There are some things in your life you

need to straighten out." At that moment, He took it away. The grieving was gone forever. The words God spoke were so plain and clear. It was as if He was actually standing before me, speaking in person.

Afterward, I really felt guilty for my behavior. God was trying so hard to let me know He was there by my side, and He would bring me through the situation. I was pushing Him aside, trying to do it on my own.

The Bible tells me I can do nothing of myself. But, "I can do all things through Christ which strengtheneth me," (Phil. 4:13). I say to you, whatever difficult crisis you are experiencing today, turn it over to God, and let Him work it out, and He will. That is a fact. I had to learn the hard way.

I decided to retire from my job in 1985 and return to college. However, I did a little more traveling in between and after my college years.

My husband left me with three teenage sons to finish raising and training. Back at that time, the drugs had been dropped off into the black community in order to get rid of black men so the white man could have control of the white woman and the black woman. This was told to my sociology class by a white instructor. Our young black men fell for this trap like a ton of bricks. They wanted that fast money. They stopped going to school, they got hooked on using the drugs, they ended up in prison, and many of them were killed.

I desperately wanted to help our young black men, and at the same time, keep track of what was going on with my sons. I decided to pursue a career in substance abuse counseling at Highland Park Community College. I received an associate degree in May of 1991.

However, I'm still traveling.

I went to Bermuda on July 19–26, 1992, with Robert E. Johnson Sr. and the Wolverine Pathfinders of the Sharon SDA Church. The people were kind and friendly. I had never seen any blue waters or oceans before. It was quite an exciting experience.

I went on a cruise to Alaska by ship in July of 1993. We were basically surrounded by water. It was interesting to see that part of the world and its inhabitants, the animals, and also sea animals.

I also went to Atlanta, Georgia, in 1994 with some of my church members to attend the King's Daughters Federation Convention Oct. 26–30. We were all members of the organization. I also got to visit Dr. Martin Luther King Jr.'s tomb site.

I was still working in my church as a deaconess. I was working with the Sabbath School Department and also singing in the Senior Choir. However, God apparently had another calling on my life. Back in 1990, God warned me in a very clear dream that I should get into the ministry. I was awakened with these words: "Even your children will not be saved until you get into the ministry." I thought about the text found in Isaiah 49:25: "I will contend with him that contendeth with thee, and I will save thy children." I was so disturbed by the dream that, right away, I shared it with my daughter-in-law, Delores. Later, I shared it with my pastor, Elder Robinson. He said, "Sister, it sounds as though God is calling you, but there are different areas of ministry." I was waiting for God to reveal to me which area of the ministry He wanted me to pursue. I wondered, is the Lord calling me to preach?

> *There are different areas of ministry.*

I am still witnessing for the Lord on a personal level. First of all, back in the day, I witnessed to my dad about God's true Sabbath and the keeping of the commandments. I share the same with my siblings, my immediate family, my neighbors, friends, and those who come into my home for repairs and improvement or for whatever reason. I give books to those who like to read. *The Great Controversy* by E.G. White, *Ten Commandments Twice Removed* by Danny Shelton, and whatever Bible-based books I have on hand at that time. This is one way that I witness for God even unto this present day.

Back in 1978, I listened quite often to the minister Jim Bakker through his broadcasting station, the PTL Club in Charlotte, North Carolina. One day, the Holy Spirit spoke to me about witnessing to him regarding the Sabbath through a letter. I thought, *no, I can't do that. This minister knows the Bible far better than me.* It kept coming to my mind if this minister could be reached, thousands and thousands of people would be directed to the right path for their spiritual life. Through the continual prompting of the Holy Spirit, I picked up my pen to write. God gave me every word that I wrote in this letter. The very day that I completed the letter, I received a book in the mail from the Voice of Prophecy ministry regarding the keeping of the Sabbath and God's commandments. I put the book in with the letter and mailed it to Jim Bakker. Sad to say, a few years later, I heard that his ministry had fallen apart.

During the time I had the dream regarding the ministry, I was counseling our young black men who had become addicted to drugs. Actually, I worked with them for two years. I couldn't tolerate it any longer. It broke my heart when they suddenly relapsed after recovering and seemingly doing so well. It was a back-and-forth situation, truly heartbreaking.

I'm still on the go, traveling. In October of the year 2000, I revisited Oakwood College in Huntsville, Alabama, for a weekend King's Daughters Federation Convention. What a blessing to set foot on the ground where I found the direction for my life according to the Bible. Yes, I will tell anyone; they are holy grounds. I could feel and sense the same sacredness that I felt in 1947 when I first stepped on those grounds.

I also visited Spain in November of the year 2000. I spent nine days in different cities of Spain. It is the most beautiful country that I have seen so far with its blossoming trees and flowers all around. They also have lots of beautiful cut flowers inside the buildings. Spain is noted for its huge Catholic cathedrals and a huge winery, which we all could probably do better without, right?

STAGE 5

From Older Adult Forward

Can you imagine? In October 2002, I was stopped in my tracks in a head-on auto collision. I was on my way to another King's Daughters Federation Conference held in the state of Indiana, along with some of my church members who were also members of this organization. I was traveling with a longtime friend, Catherine Neal, whom I met when I left Oakwood College and came to Detroit, Michigan. She was trailing the other group from my church, and instantly, the brakes on her car stopped functioning. She had absolutely no control of the automobile. She had to choose whether to go down the steep cliff to the right side of the highway, or ram into the back of the car that she was trailing, or go to the left and meet head-on with the oncoming traffic. That is exactly what happened.

We were taken to the nearest emergency hospital to evaluate our injuries. I had a broken right leg and a broken left arm. My injuries were more severe than my friend's, the driver of the car.

I could have been killed in this head-on auto collision; however, God saw fit to preserve my life for a specific reason. He tells us in this word, Psalm 121, verse 8, "The Lord shall preserve thy going out and thy coming in from this time forth, and even for evermore."

During my recovery period of two months in a rehab facility, I prayed to God continually, read, and studied His Word along with E.G. White's writings. It was revealed to me that I was to become involved in the ministry of literature evangelism. Sometimes God has to break us in order to make us, right? God tells us in Matthew 28:19–20, "Go ye therefore, and teach all nations, baptizing them in the name of the Father, and of the Son, and of the Holy Ghost: Teaching them to observe all things whatsoever I have commanded you: and, lo, I am with you always, even unto the end of the world. Amen."

Believe me, that's what it is all about, witnessing and winning souls for Christ. When I stand in the judgment before God, and He asks me, "Where is that beautiful flock I have entrusted unto you?" I want to be able to look around and say, "Lord, here they are." I want to see you there along with all of God's people who are there as a result of my witnessing to them in whatever way.

Just follow God's way for your life according to the Bible, and do not follow the way of the world. You will have perfect peace of mind, and it will be well with your soul. It is just that simple.

After recovering from the auto accident, I started working with Brother James Jones, who was the leader of the evangelistic department in my church through the Lake Region Conference. I also attended different seminars pertaining to evangelism and witnessing. I found out how very important and urgent it is for us as a church body to go out into the community from door to door and spread the gospel of Jesus Christ and the three angels' messages to a sinful and dying world; to prepare them for the second appearing of Christ.

It is people and their salvation that matters most. "If there is any one thing in the world in which we may manifest enthusiasm, it may be manifested in seeking the salvation of the souls for whom Christ died" (*Selected Messages*, vol. 1, p. 139).

After the passing away of Brother James Jones, I took over his position as head of the evangelistic department in my church. I ordered tons of the book *Ten Commandments Twice Removed* from 3ABN. I urged my church family to get active in giving out the books in whatever way possible. Give them to family members, to neighbors, to co-workers, and mail them to people whom they know.

Linda Robinson, dedicated worker for God, and I would spend time each Sabbath after church service going from door to door handing out these books. Finally, Pastor Phillip Jones decided to close out the eleven o'clock service a few times on the Sabbath and have the whole church body, except the ones who were unable to do a lot of walking, go out into the community from door to door and give out the books. Those who were unable to go out stayed at the church and sent up prayers to God for the ones who went out. That was quite an exciting experience.

During this time, I was still going from door to door in my immediate neighborhood on Sundays with the help of my grandchildren. When I didn't have their help, I would occasionally go out alone to give out the books.

One specific Sunday, I was motivated to go out, but I was skeptical about going out alone. The Holy Spirit kept prompting me, and I obeyed. The second door that I knocked on, I found out the young man living there was from my home state, North Carolina, and the town that's ten miles from my hometown. I gave him the book, witnessed to him regarding the keeping of the Sabbath, and invited him to church. He did attend my church at one time. However, I found out he had severe back problems as a result of his construction work for years. Sad to say, he passed away shortly after my coming in contact with him. Apparently, the Lord wanted me to contact this young man.

During these years of evangelistic work in the church and on a personal level, I was also attending college. After giving up on substance abuse counseling, I went back to school to study a career in gerontology. I have always preferred working with older people rather than children. I can relate to them better than to children. Older people seem to be more appreciative of what you do for them. For the most part, they are kind, they are genuine, they are interesting, and I learn a lot from them. Older people also make good friends. They have given their all to their family and to society. They deserve the very best.

I graduated from Wayne County Community College in 1997 with an associate degree in gerontology. I was an honor graduate and also inducted into the Phi Theta Kappa Society in 1998.

I attribute my success first of all to God, whom I prayed to continually, and my favorite scripture that I focused on and repeated often. "I can do all things through Christ which strengtheneth me" (Phil. 4:13).

Secondly, I attribute my success to Dr. Catherine Wells, who was my gerontology instructor. She was a warm and caring person. She insisted that you feel good about yourself and who you are. I explained to her the problem I had in speaking out and speaking before an audience or group of people. She worked diligently with me, trying to resolve the problem by having me stand before the class and speak on different topics related to gerontology. She would always say, "Bernette, you did an excellent job." She was a very encouraging and inspiring person. She believed the more you use your brain and keep your mind activated, the less likely you are to attract Alzheimer's disease and other brain-deteriorating diseases. She also felt that it was never too late to get an education and make changes in your life for the better.

With the help of Dr. Wells and the fact that I took two extra speech classes while in college, I was able to overcome the quietness and was enabled to express myself better and have the courage to speak before an audience.

Guess what? After taking those two extra speech classes, I told the children's story at my church's eleven o'clock Sabbath service for the first time.

A couple, a man and his wife who were members of my church, moved to the state of West Virginia after his retirement. They came back to visit their original hometown, and they attended church on the Sabbath that I told the children's story. I spoke to the man after the service was over. He congratulated me on the storytelling. I said, "Praise the Lord." He then said, "I thought to myself, this lady doesn't even talk, and she's up there telling the children's story!" He said, "The Holy Spirit can do wonders." I said, "That is very true.".

After graduation from W.C.C. College, I was hired at Heartland Health Care Center in Dearborn Heights, Michigan, as an activity assistant. I enjoyed planning different programs to occupy the senior citizens during their leisure time. During some of the different programs, I was also able to witness to them regarding the Sabbath and keeping of the commandments of God. At one point, I invited the youth from my church to come and present a singing program. Working with the seniors was truly an exciting and rewarding experience.

During the time I worked at Heartland Health Care Center is when I was caught up in the automobile accident. I was unable to recover and restore my body to be able to fulfill all the requirements of the job. So, I had to retire.

However, during my work time at Heartland, I was a recipient of the Ability is Ageless, Most ABLE Award and trophy that was presented to me at the Eighth Annual Operation ABLE Ability is Ageless Awards and Luncheon held on October 30, 1997, at the Hyatt Regency in Dearborn, Michigan, for what they considered outstanding work.

After recovery from the accident, I decided to go back to visit my hometown of Murfreesboro, North Carolina, in August of 2003. At this time, I was also invited to attend my high school reunion held on August 29–30 at C.S. Brown High School in Winton, North Carolina. It was truly a blessing to attend the reunion and get to see and meet with some of my former classmates and friends whom I had not seen since graduating from high school.

It was also amazing to see the Chowan College campus flooded with African-American students at this time. I was restrained from attending this college when I finished high school. Yes, because of the color of my skin. Segregation in schools ended during President Dwight D. Eisenhower's term: 1953–1961, along with the help of President John F. Kennedy, who helped to pass laws regarding the Civil Rights Movement during the 1960s. It was a great pleasure to learn that things had changed.

My youngest sister, Ruth Esther, who lived in Hollis, New York, also came down for the school reunion. We were able to stay in a hotel there in our town during our time there without any restrictions or segregation, which was altogether different in times past.

The most exciting of all was, we were able to go out to the farm where we were born and grew up on. I was happy to see and set foot on the grounds that were my childhood experience. We visited the country elementary school that we attended when we first started school at six years of age. The school was not occupied but still standing. We were able to see and visit the entire community surrounding the farm and visit with some of the neighbors that were still alive.

We were also able to visit the home church that we grew up attending as children. It was a blessing to see some of the older members still there. The entire trip was surely a rewarding and invigorating experience.

However, in getting back home safely, I thought, *It's time to put a damper on traveling. It's time to do more work for God, working in the church and spreading the gospel of Jesus Christ to the world.* I believe the auto accident was my wake-up call. In spite of all that was happening, I was inspired to take one more trip abroad.

In November of the year 2003, I decided to take a trip to Australia with some of my church members. We spent eleven days there. Most of our time was spent in Melbourne and Sydney. During our visit to Sydney one evening, we viewed the city from above as we dined at a revolving restaurant. We also visited the Sydney Opera House, and we visited the Koala Park and saw the koalas, the kangaroos, and wombats.

We were also able to make contact and communicate with the Aborigines of the country. I enjoyed the beautiful country of Australia immensely. The air was fresh and clean, along with the many waterfalls. What an exciting adventure!

My traveling days are over until I travel seven days from earth to heaven, according to E.G. White, with Jesus Christ, when He comes to take His people home to live with Him forever.

I want to do what the Lord wants me to do. I want to be who He wants me to be. After I resigned from the position as head of the evangelistic department, I joined hands with Dr. Pola Hall, who took over the position. She truly has a passion for reaching souls for Christ. We were constantly on the go, along with two other individuals, who joined with us until the pandemic stopped us dead in our tracks. We went out in different areas surrounding our church and the city of Inkster, Michigan.

Her schedule was to go out into the community from door to door on Sunday for at least two hours or more during the spring into the summer and early fall of the year.

After our introduction, Dr. Hall's mission was to find out the person's specific needs and find out if they had any medical problems or if they had any concerns about high blood pressure. If so, she would take it and give them the reading. If they desired prayer for any specific reason or just prayer in general, we would do that. We would also tell them about the food pantry at our church if they or anyone they knew needed food. We presented them with the schedule of the days and time to pick it up and the location of our church, the phone number, and all the needed information. We also invited them to our church service if they weren't attending any church.

Finally, we gave them a book to read regarding questions and answers to the Bible and also tracks and pamphlets on overcoming diabetes and different diseases and addictions. If I discovered someone really liked to read, I would give them the book *Ten Commandments Twice Removed* by Danny Shelton and Shelly Quinn.

After the coronavirus pandemic began, our door-to-door contact was put on hold. Dr. Hall decided to have me write a five-minute script on diet and foods or keeping the commandments of God to post on her mobile device to go out to social media. I chose the diet and foods script, recognizing God is just as concerned about our physical health as He is about our spiritual wellbeing. In 3 John 2, He tells us, "Beloved, I wish above all things that thou mayest prosper and be in health, even as thy soul prospereth."

We have to be aware of what we eat if we want to live a long, healthy life. The original diet that we had when God created us was fruits, vegetables, and grains. He did not create our bodies to consume animals. Only after the flood, God consented for man to eat only the clean meats. Check Leviticus chapter 11.

Now, at this time in world history, the clean meats have become unclean. "There is an increase of disease in the animal kingdom. The meat you eat is contaminated and infected to a degree never before known in human history." (*International Meat Crisis* by Vance Ferrell.)

After eating the flesh of the diseased animals, we take on their disease in our tissue and blood, and when we are exposed to prevailing epidemics or the coronavirus pandemic and other contagious diseases, our body cannot resist the disease.

There will be no flesh food or meat in heaven. We should start getting rid of it now while upon the earth, so we can live life to the fullest. Amen?

Getting back to my witnessing, at the beginning of the coronavirus pandemic, I also bonded with 3ABN in mailing out the COVID-19 books to my zip code area, which was a blessing to be able to reach God's people in this way.

While we are reaching out to others, we have to continue witnessing to our own individual families and deal with the issues and problems that they are experiencing. It is not an easy task. For the most part, they don't really want to hear my side of the story. They want to do things their way or follow the way of the world and expect God to pour out His blessings upon them.

I have to remember to be patient with family members, just as God has been patient with me. The Bible tells us, we were all born in sin and shaped in iniquity. We come here prone to go with the way of the world.

I have been going through some tough struggles with my family ever since my husband passed away in 1984. My oldest son, Quinton, decided to quit college at the age of nineteen and unite in marriage. During the early years of his marriage, his wife's brother-in-law introduced him to the usage of drugs, and that became an ongoing habit for the rest of his years. The drugs took complete control of his life. However, he continued to work for Ford Motor Co. until the drugs had destroyed his body. During the year of 2012, his illness escalated to the point that he had to take time off from his job and go through different medical treatments. Finally, he had to be hospitalized.

I was constantly praying for him every day throughout the entire day. One specific day, I was praying for him, and the Lord spoke and gave me a short sinner's prayer. As the words were revealed to me, I wrote them down on a notepad and laid it aside and thought no more about it.

The prayer was: "My God and my Father, who art in heaven, will You please take my heart and change my life, and I am yours forever. Thank You, Lord, for forgiving me of all my sins and saving my soul eternally with You. Thank You in Jesus' name, amen."

On a Sunday morning in mid-July of 2012, I was praying for him and contemplating on the best time to visit him. I thought perhaps I should visit him at lunchtime and try to encourage him to eat his food because he had been refusing to eat because he didn't like the way the food tasted. During this time, the Lord spoke to me and said, "Take that prayer I gave you and read it to your son and then have him repeat it after you." I said, "Yes, Lord, I can do that." I didn't even know where it was. I had to search through different notepads and papers. I finally found it.

When I arrived at the hospital, his caregiver had been there and had given him a bath and put a nice warm robe on him because he was always complaining of being cold. He was glowing and sparkling. He looked extremely good. He didn't look at all like he was sick.

He had finished eating his food, and he was drinking his liquids. So, I said, "Quinton, I have a prayer I want to read to you, and after I read it, I want you to repeat it after me." He agreed. After this was completed, I told him to put the prayer into the drawer of his bedside table, and he could repeat it at any time.

> *He was glowing and sparkling. He looked extremely good. He didn't look at all like he was sick.*

Can you imagine? During the late Sunday evening hours, according to his nurse, his blood count went out of control, and they could not bring it back to normal. Sad to say, he went into a coma, and he passed away on July 10, 2012.

I say to you, we have an awesome God. He will do everything to save us no matter how far we stray from Him. God will make a way of escape if we will humbly submit ourselves to Him and ask for His forgiveness. My son Quinton's experience was similar to the thief on the cross's experience; a last-minute acceptance of God in his life. Thank God for saving both of them eternally with Him.

I thanked God for hearing my prayers and making a way for my son to speak for himself. Even though I had been continually praying for him, God had to hear the words from the mouth of Quinton, asking for forgiveness for all of his sins and to be saved eternally. "I will contend with him that contendeth with thee, and I will save thy children" (Isa. 49:25).

As you continue to follow my journey, the road becomes even more rugged. My second son, Durwin, also became caught up in the usage of drugs as a teenager. He insisted on doing things his way. It was truly heartbreaking; however, I could not cast him aside even though I did not like what he was doing. I have striven to live a godly life before my family and set the right example. They no longer have their father, no grandparents, and no uncles left to help encourage and direct them in the right direction.

I prayed for Durwin constantly, asking God to step in and take control of his life. I asked God to take away the taste and the desire for the ungodly things of this world—drugs, chemicals, cigarettes—whatever Satan had him bound up in.

I recognize we cannot pull our loved ones and family members out of their addiction and ungodly habits. We have to pray them out of their situation. At times it seems as though it is a losing battle. We have to be persistent in prayer, show kindness, mercy, and trust God to deliver them. We have to also remember we're not dealing with the actual person; we are dealing with whom the drugs have made them to become. The drugs are in control. We cannot give up on them or turn our backs on them; otherwise, they will not win the battle. Satan will gain total and complete control.

I prayed for Durwin twenty-seven years before he made up his mind to let go and let God take charge of his life. He was baptized on May 21, 2011, at my church, the Sharon SDA Church in Inkster, Michigan. Durwin overcame with the help of God, a renewed person in Christ Jesus in spite of Satan and all of his trickery.

He loved reading and studying the Bible and reading E.G. White's books. Sad to say, he, Durwin, was put to sleep in Christ Jesus on September 13, 2016.

If you have been praying for a family member, friend, or neighbor to surrender their life to God and you have not yet gotten visible results, my suggestion to you is to keep on praying for them. God will come through in due time. There is no problem too great, no problem too small for God to solve, and we can never underestimate the power of God.

I talk, witness, and give counsel to my family whenever the opportunity presents itself to let them know I care deeply about them. "I love you." I'm your mother, your grandmother, auntie, whatever the case might be. "I will never stop loving you." "You are my flesh and blood." "I desire the best for you, and so does God."

However, the road on my journey gets more rough and rugged as we continue. Can you imagine? My grandson, Andrea, who was Durwin's oldest son, was killed in a motorcycle accident on August 20, 2019. He was forty years of age but had not completely given himself over to God. He was brought up and trained in the right way according to the Bible at an early age.

I started taking Andrea and one of his cousins, Dajuan, to church when they both were five years old. As a matter of fact, I took most of my grandchildren and great-grandchildren to church starting at an early age. However, when they became teenagers, they decided they wanted to do their own thing. I could not force them to continue attending church because I'm the grandmother, not the mother, of course, nor the father. It broke my heart because I felt that the teen years was the time or age that they really needed to be rooted and grounded into the church.

The Bible tells us, "Train up a child in the way he should go: and when he is old, he will not depart from it" (Prov. 22:6). Andrea attended church occasionally; however, I was praying and waiting on him to come back and surrender all to God.

Andrea was not killed instantly in the accident. He was taken to the nearest hospital emergency unit, and he passed away shortly afterward. My hope is that he remembered and had the time to say, "Lord, please save me."

The next shocking fact is, Andrea's brother, Jermaine, came up to Detroit, Michigan, from the state of Mississippi to attend Andrea's funeral. During his time in Detroit, on one specific day, Jermaine went to a restaurant for his evening meal. During this time, his family members were trying to contact him by phone. No one understood why he was not answering his phone. After checking things out, his mother finally discovered that the police department had found Jermaine dead in his car in the restaurant's parking lot. Apparently, he was so disturbed and grief-stricken over his brother's death that he had a heart attack at the age of thirty-nine years young on August. 28, 2019, eight days after his brother Andrea's death.

I was indeed shocked about what had happened to Jermaine. I'm thinking to myself, *what is next?* Shortly after the tragedy of my grandsons, Katherine Neal's daughter, Joan called and informed me that her mother had passed away in her sleep on September 4, 2019. Sad to say, that was next. Katherine was ninety-four years young.

I met Katherine Neal when I came to Detroit, Michigan, from Oakwood College. At that time, her name was Katherine Cole. She came from Emmanuel Missionary College to Detroit. It is now known as Andrews

University. We both came to Detroit as students to sell magazines and evangelistic books in order to earn a scholarship for college.

We both worked under the supervision of the same person who was head of the evangelistic department in the Detroit area at that time. This is when I first met Katherine. I found her to be the most godly, Christian young woman that I had ever met. She was kind, and she always spoke encouraging words to me, directing me in the right direction. Katherine was like my blood sister. She was truly a Christian mentor for me from the time I met her until she slept away. She also enabled me to overcome my Southern accent. She was good at helping me pronounce words correctly.

Katherine did not return to Emmanuel Missionary College. However, in her later years, she returned to college and earned a bachelor's degree and a master's in education and sociology from Wayne State University. Katherine taught school in the Detroit public school system for twenty years. Most of all, she was a godly Adventist Christian who believed in living her life according to the Bible. I regret not being able to see her or make contact with her.

In spite of all that has happened, sadly, I also have to inform you that my youngest sister, Ruth Esther, the youngest of all of my siblings, passed away on March 11, 2020, prior to the spreading of the coronavirus. She was ninety years young. She was diagnosed as having an e-Coli infection.

We grew up together on a country farm. We worked together, we played together, we went to church together. We even sang in church together in a family group of three. We always bonded together well from childhood until her death. She resided in Hollis, New York. She was a mother of two sons. She worked as a probation officer in New York City for most of her working years.

I visited Esther quite often when my children were youngsters. We would stay up late at night going through the Bible so she could see herself that what I had been witnessing to her about the Sabbath and keeping the commandments of God came directly from the Bible. Actually, I had been witnessing to my sister from the time I came into the knowledge of the real truth of the Bible at Oakwood College. I would also send her the *Message* magazine and different books written by E.G. White at intervals.

I have also been witnessing to Esther's son Freddie, who lived with her and was her dedicated caretaker. I shared with him how he could get information regarding the Sabbath through SabbathTruth.com on his cellphone. I also sent him various texts taken from the New Testament regarding the Sabbath.

Can you imagine? The last time I talked with my sister over the phone shortly before her death, she said, "Bernette, I have made up my mind to live my life strictly by the Bible." At least, she had made up her mind, although she wasn't able to follow through with her decision. We have an awesome God. Amen?

After all the trials and sadness that I have endured since and with the passing of my husband in 1984 until the death of my sister in 2020, I cannot complain. However, I can truly say, God is good; not sometime, but all of the time, God is good. God brought me through all of those difficult situations after learning to turn the problems over to Him and pray continually to Him to take complete control of the situation and work it out, according to His will. I ask the Lord to lift my spirit, lift my courage, and may Satan not have the victory. I also ask God to give me the faith to know that He will bring me through. Lord, you have told me in your word, "Ask, and it shall be given you; seek, and ye shall find; knock, and it shall be opened unto you" (Matt. 7:7). Prayer is the key to whatever problem or situation that confronts us from day to day.

We also have to remember, when we lose a family member, sibling, or loved one, we have to recognize this world is not our home. After Adam and Eve sinned in the Garden of Eden by eating the forbidden fruit, we have been in big-time trouble ever since. We are all going to die one day; we just don't know when. If we knew when, we would worry ourselves to death. Right? Now that we know we're going to leave this planet Earth sooner or later, the key is to live our lives in total, complete harmony with God's will according to the Bible. Then, we can get to live with all of our family members, siblings, and loved ones who choose to be saved forever in eternity in perfect bodies—no pain, no suffering, or crying (see Rev. 21:4, Isa. 33:24). If we live one hundred years or more upon this earth, it can never compare to living forever in eternity. Forever?? That is mind-boggling!

I pray that this journey has not been boring or disgusting to you. Instead, I trust that it will inspire you to surrender your life over to God and go all the way with Him, according to the Bible.

We have to abandon our own opinions and how we feel about God and His word. We should ask God to reveal His truth to us. Do not trust the word of others. There are so many educated people that rely on their pastor or minister to give them the truth of God's Word rather than reading it for themselves. It seems as if the more educated the person is, the harder it is to reach them with the Word of God. Jesus chose uneducated, ordinary men to be His disciples because they were humble and teachable men, who didn't think they knew it all. God could reach them and teach them.

When it's all said and done, God is the only One who can save us. Why do we rely on others' words instead of God's Word? People cannot save themselves, so how can they save us?

The Bible tells us that those who teach contrary to God's Word and lead others down the wrong path will definitely be held accountable. In the end, God will say to them, "I never knew you: depart from me, ye that work iniquity" (Matt. 7:22–23).

THE CONCLUSION

This whole Christian walk is a controversy between God and Satan, good and evil, right and wrong. It is totally up to each of us to decide which path we're going to take. Satan is powerful, but God is all-powerful. God is merciful; He is patient, kind, longsuffering, and forgiving. God does not bang us over our head and say, "Come on; do things My way." He gives us freedom of choice. He tells us in His Word, "If you love me, keep my commandments" (John 14:15, NKJV). God wants us to follow Him because of love and not because of force or fear.

God did not destroy Satan from the beginning of his fall because the angels and the whole universe would have served God because of fear instead of love. Joshua states, "And if it seem evil unto you to serve the Lord, choose for yourselves this day whom you will serve … but as for me and my house, we will serve the Lord" (Josh. 24:15, NKJV).

"For God sent not his Son into the world to condemn the world; but that the world through Him might be saved" (John 3:17).

On the contrary, Satan wants to destroy all of us in whatever way he can—dead in our sins. Thank God, Satan is a defeated foe. He was defeated at the cross when Jesus Christ, God's only begotten Son, came from the riches of heaven to this sinful world and shed His blood on a cruel cross for you and me and the whole world. Let us take advantage of the price that Jesus has paid for our sins through His precious blood.

Let us make up our mind to go all the way with God, according to the Bible. Let us remember the Sabbath day to keep it holy and keep all of God's commandments, the whole law of God.

"Blessed are they that do His commandments, that they may have right to the tree of life, and may enter in through the gates into the city" (Rev. 22:14). I truly want to enter in through the gates into that city that He has prepared for me. What about you?!

God is trying to wake us up and let us know that Jesus Christ is coming soon. I would like to read a passage from E.G. White's writings from *Testimonies for the Church*, vol. 9, p. 11. She talks about the things that will be happening in the world just before the second coming of Jesus. She states, there will be economic crises, loss of jobs, loss of homes, increase in crimes, disasters by land and sea, turbulent weather, raging fires. All of this and more has been happening before our eyes every day all across the U.S. and the world. It is time for us to sound the trumpet and loud let it ring. Jesus is coming again and soon.

God is calling His people to awaken and come out of Babylon. "Babylon is fallen" (Rev. 14:8). Babylon is considered false worship. "Come out of her, my people, that ye be not partakers of her sins, and that ye receive not of her plagues" (Rev. 18:4).

I am pleading to you to come join with me and honor and obey God. Walk in the way that He has commissioned you by keeping all of His commandments and remembering the Sabbath day, the seventh day, not the first day, to keep it holy. "And other sheep I have, which are not of this fold: them also I must bring, and they shall hear my voice; and there shall be one fold, and one shepherd" (John 10:16).

I can never, never thank God enough for directing me into the right path and bringing me into the knowledge of His Word, the Bible, and His will for my life. He will do the same for you or anyone who is truly seeking to know God, His Word, and His will for their life. God has His own unique way of reaching each of us. We only have to sincerely desire to know Him and His will for us. God will reveal it to you in His own way, in His own time. He did it for me, and He will do it for you.

With all of the trials and brokenness we have to endure in this world, we wonder if God can use us to reach His people to witness for Him. He uses the broken to reach the brokenhearted, just as He uses broken clouds to produce rain to produce grain.

Weeping may endure for a moment, but joy cometh in the morning. I look forward to seeing and meeting with you in Heaven.

Praise the Lord forever and ever more. Alleluia, Alleluia, Amen, Amen.

May the grace of our Lord Jesus Christ be with you all forever and ever. Amen, Amen, Amen.

With Love,

Bernette

I. <u>Obey</u> God's Commandments and live forever.

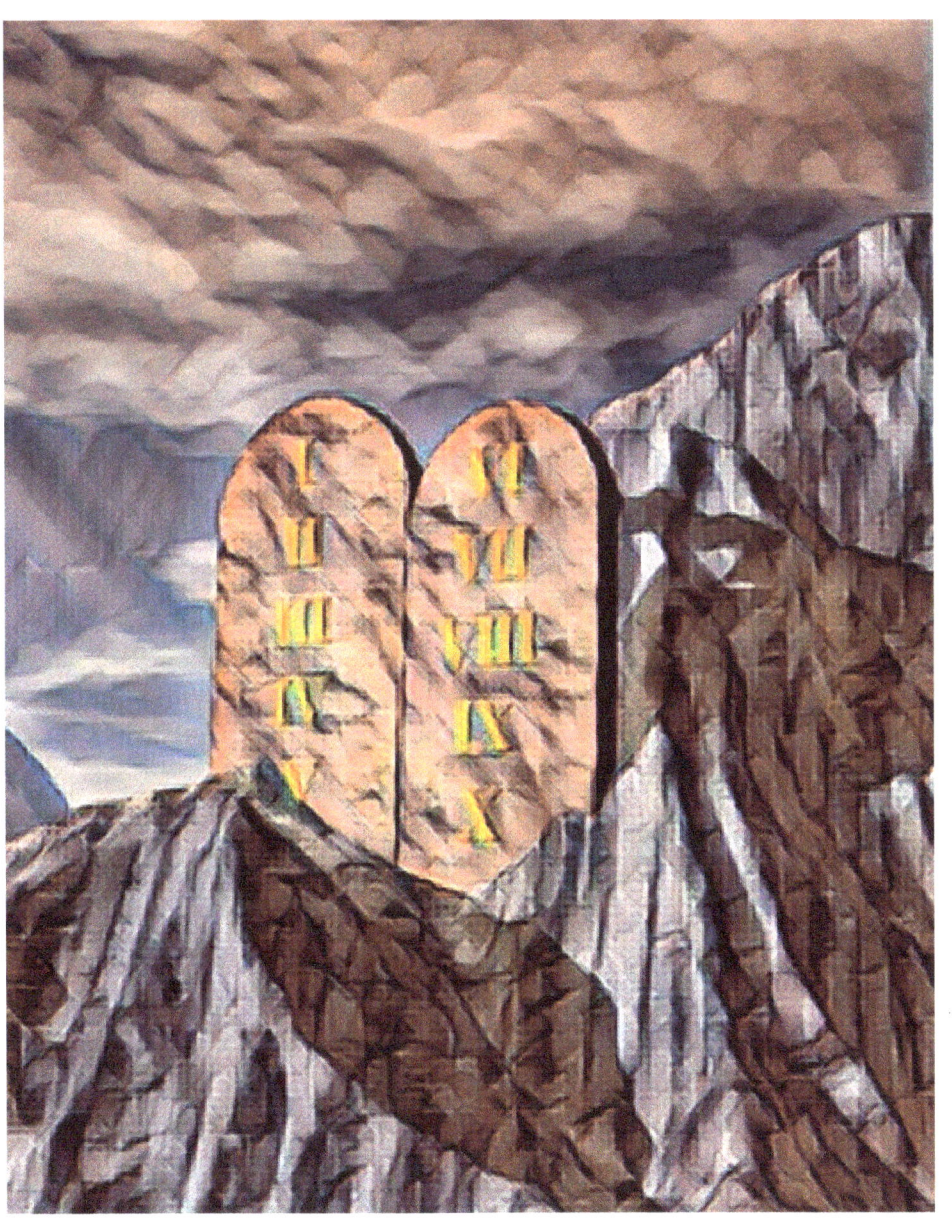

II. <u>Disobey</u> and be destroyed in the lake of fire with Satan and his unholy angels.

I don't know about you, but I want to live forever in Heaven with God the Father and Jesus Christ His Son. Amen.

ASPECT Books

We invite you to view the complete
selection of titles we publish at:
www.ASPECTBooks.com

We encourage you to write us
with your thoughts about this,
or any other book we publish at:
info@ASPECTBooks.com

ASPECT Books' titles may be purchased in
bulk quantities for educational, fund-raising,
business, or promotional use.
bulksales@ASPECTBooks.com

Finally, if you are interested in seeing
your own book in print, please contact us at:
publishing@ASPECTBooks.com
We are happy to review your manuscript at no charge.

www.ingramcontent.com/pod-product-compliance
Lightning Source LLC
Chambersburg PA
CBHW040313170426
43195CB00020B/2963